THE WORLD
IN THE TIME OF
LEONARDO DA VINCI

Chelsea House Publishers
Philadelphia

FIONA MACDONALD

First published in hardback edition in 2001
by Chelsea House Publishers, a subsidiary of
Haights Cross Communications. All rights reserved.
Printed and bound in China.

First published in the UK in 1997 by
Belitha Press Limited, London House,
Great Eastern Wharf, Parkgate Road,
London SW11 4NQ, England

Text by Fiona Macdonald
Map by Robin Carter, Wildlife Art Agency

Editor: Claire Edwards
Art Director: Helen James
Design: Ros Saunders
Picture Researcher: Diana Morris
Consultant: Sallie Purkiss

First printing
1 3 5 7 9 8 6 4 2

The Chelsea House World Wide Web address is:
http://www.chelseahouse.com

Library of Congress Cataloging-in-Publication Data applied for.

ISBN: 0-7910-6032-2

Printed in Hong Kong
9 8 7 6 5 4 3 2 1

Picture acknowledgements: AKG, London: 4 Biblioteca Reale, Turin.
Bridgeman Art Library: front cover l British Library, London;
back cover British Museum, London; 1cl St Peter's Vatican Collection;
1cr Giraudon/Biblioteca Nacional, Madrid; 2 American Museum of Natural
History, New York; 5t Museo di Firenze Com'era; 6b Bibliothèque de
l'Institut de France, Paris; 12 Bibliothèque Nationale, Paris;
14b British Museum, London; 16 British Library, London; 17b
Biblioteca Nacional, Madrid; 19b Palazzo Medici-Riccardi, Florence;
22t Victoria & Albert Museum, London; 22b Royal Geographical
Society, London; 23r Giraudon/Biblioteca Nacional, Madrid; 25t
British Library, London; 28 National Library of Australia, Canberra;
29t British Museum, London; 29b American Museum of Natural History,
New York; 30 Stapleton College; 31t Raymond O'Shea Gallery, London;
31b British Library, London; 32b Chester Beatty Library, Dublin; 34 Victoria &
Albert Museum, London; 36 St Peter's Vatican Collection; 37t National Gallery,
London; 37b **Bridgeman Art Library**: Uffizi Gallery, Florence; 38l British
Library, London; 39t, 40b, 41t, 41c, 45l British Museum, London. **British
Museum, London**: 5b. **E.T. Archive**: 3 Louvre, Paris; 6t Czartorysky Museum,
Cracow; 7b Louvre, Paris; 13 Moldovita Monstery, Romania; 17t University
Museum, Cuzco; 18 El Prado, Madrid; 19t British Museum, London;

Picture acknowledgments cont: 23l Pedro de Osma Museum, Lima; 24
Torre Aquila, Trento; 25b University Library, Istanbul; 35t; 42 National Museum,
Copenhagen. **Werner Forman Archive**: 1c British Museum, London;
15 Kuroda Collection, Japan; 20r British Museum, London; 26t; 33 Kozu
Collection, Kyoto; 39b Private Collection; 45r Biblioteca Universitaria,
Bologna. **Sonia Halliday Photographs**: 20l Topkapi Palace Museum, Istanbul;
26b James Wellard; 38r. **Robert Harding Picture Library**: 21t Schuster;
44 Michael Jenner. **Copyright reserved to HM The Queen**: 7t. **Michael
Holford**: 43. **Images of India**: 40t N.M. Kelva. **Japan Archive**: 21b. **N.J.
Saunders**: 35b. **Scala**: front cover r. **Topkapi Palace Museum, Istanbul**:
32t. **University of Tokyo**: 27.

CONTENTS

ABOUT THIS BOOK

This book tells the story of Leonardo da Vinci and also looks at what was happening all around the world in his time. To help you find your way through the book, each chapter has been divided into seven sections. Each section describes a different part of the world and is headed by a color bar. As you look through a chapter, the color bars tell you which area you can read about in the text below. There is a time line, to give you an outline of world events in Leonardo's time, and also a map, which shows some of the most important places mentioned in the book.

On page 46 is a list of some of the peoples you will read about in this book. Some of the more unfamiliar words are also listed in the glossary.

THE STORY OF LEONARDO

▲ Leonardo painted this picture of a serious and thoughtful old man when he himself was getting old. As with the picture of Leonardo on the cover, people think that this is a self-portrait, but no one knows for sure.

Leonardo da Vinci was born more than 500 years ago, but his name is still remembered today, and his achievements are admired all around the world. No one else in Leonardo's time studied so many different topics and had so many brilliant ideas. This book tells you a little about his life as an artist, a scientist, and an engineer. It also tells you what was happening elsewhere in the world in Leonardo's time.

Leonardo lived from 1452 to 1519, but this book covers a longer time span, from about 1450 to 1550. It will help you to find out about events that shaped the world before Leonardo was born and to discover what happened in the years after he died.

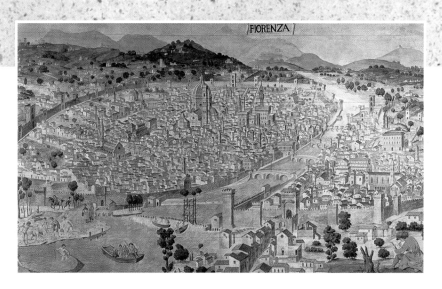

A DIFFICULT START

Leonardo did not have a good start in life. His mother was a peasant woman called Caterina, and his father, Ser Piero da Vinci, was a lawyer. They were not married, but Piero da Vinci took young Leonardo into his family and brought him up.

A NEW HOME IN FLORENCE

Around 1469, Leonardo moved with his father and stepmother to Florence, one of the richest and most splendid cities in Italy. Florence was a center of trade and industry, especially for fine woolen cloth. Some of Italy's richest merchants lived there, in huge palaces. They paid for new houses, churches, fountains, and gardens and filled them with wonderful pictures and statues.

▲ The city of Florence in the 1500s. It was a great business center, and many of Europe's earliest banks were set up there. Florence was governed by a rich family called the Medici. They encouraged the best artists to come and work in the city.

AN APPRENTICESHIP

Even as a child Leonardo liked drawing and was very good at it. So his father arranged for him to become an apprentice in the studio of a famous artist in Florence called Andrea del Verrocchio. An apprenticeship was the usual way for boys, and some girls, to train for a skilled craft. They went to live with a master artist or craft worker and helped with the work. In return the master fed and clothed them and taught them all his skills.

SCIENCE AND ART

For the next ten years, Leonardo worked hard. Sometimes he helped Verrocchio in his studio; sometimes he worked by himself. He studied science and engineering. He learned how to build bridges, dig canals, and design weapons. He painted, carved sculptures, and was a fine musician.

◄ Leonardo was trained in a studio like this one. In the foreground of the picture, you can see an artist entertaining a rich customer. All around you can see his assistants and apprentices designing frescoes, carving statues, and grinding colored earth to make paints.

FESTIVALS AND MAGIC MACHINES

About 1482, Leonardo moved to Milan. He went to work for the ruler, the Duke of Milan, helping to arrange festivals at the palace—with magic machines, special effects, and music. When he wasn't working for the duke, he continued with his studies. Leonardo made hundreds of sketches in his notebooks, of plants, animals, and the human body. He was fascinated to see how things fit together and how they worked.

▼ One of Leonardo's many designs for new inventions. This is a flying machine. Leonardo made detailed sketches, showing how the machine would work.

◄ While Leonardo was in Milan, he painted many pictures. This one is a portrait of the duke's friend, a fashionable Italian woman called Cecilia Gallerani. She is holding her pet ermine.

A NEW STYLE FULL OF SHADOWS

Leonardo used the information from his studies in his pictures. Stories were told about how he made collections of dead snakes, lizards, and toads so that he could paint them in a lifelike way. He concentrated so hard on his studies that he did not notice when the dead bodies began to rot and smell. Leonardo also began to develop his own way of painting at this time. People called it *sfumato*, which means "smoky." All Leonardo's people were painted in a misty, mysterious way, and his paintings were full of dark shadows.

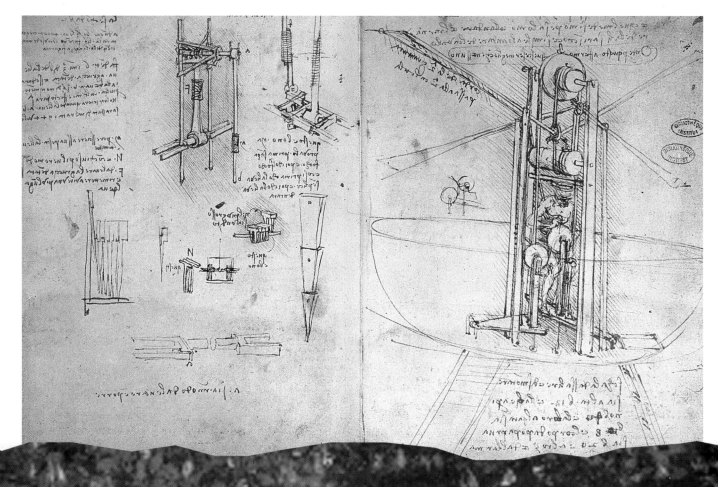

FAME IN FLORENCE

In 1500, Leonardo moved back to Florence, where he worked for the Medici family as a mapmaker and engineer and continued to paint in his own special style. By now he was very famous. At about this time, Leonardo painted his most famous portrait, called the *Mona Lisa*. It is still one of the best-known pictures in the world, although people disagree about its effect. Some call it magical and beautiful, but others find the fantasy landscape and Mona Lisa's compelling eyes and secretive smile strange and disturbing.

▲ Leonardo's most famous portrait, the *Mona Lisa*, which he painted between 1503 and 1506. Leonardo was always trying out new techniques. Here he has used such fine brushwork that you cannot see the separate strokes.

ART AND SCIENCE

In Florence, Leonardo also continued his studies. He believed that art and science should not be kept separate, but that each topic he studied would help him with all his other work. He kept a collection of notebooks (more than 3,500 pages in all) full of scientific observations and experiments. He also made sketches of his engineering designs. He wrote in backwards mirror writing, possibly to keep his notes secret, but also because he was left-handed and it was quicker and easier for him to write that way.

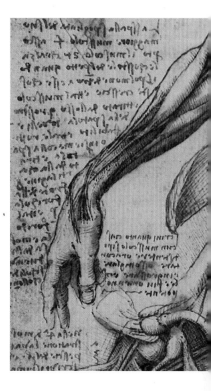

▲ A page from one of Leonardo's notebooks showing drawings of a hand, an arm, and a shoulder. Like other artists, he often cut up, then sketched, dead bodies.

WORKING FOR THE KING OF FRANCE

Between 1506 and 1513, Leonardo worked in Florence and in Milan. In 1516 he was invited by King Francis I of France to advise him on some new building plans. Francis was interested in art and admired Leonardo's work. Leonardo accepted eagerly and soon thought up all kinds of exciting new projects for the French king. These included a massive plan to control the flow of the Loire River. Leonardo died, after less than three years in France, before he could complete the plans. All over Europe people mourned him. They realized that Leonardo had been one of the most creative and inventive minds of his time.

THE WORLD 1450-1550

ABOUT THE MAPS

The maps on this page will help you find your way around the world in Leonardo da Vinci's time. The big map shows some of the places mentioned in the text, including the following:

• **COUNTRIES** that are different from modern ones, such as Persia and Benin.

• *Past peoples*, such as the Incas and Aztecs.

• *GEOGRAPHICAL FEATURES*, including mountains and rivers.

• *Towns and cities.* To find the position of a town or city, look for the name in the list below and then find the number on the map.

1 Tenochtitlán	9 Florence	15 Kilwa
2 Machu Picchu	10 Constantinople (Istanbul)	16 Samarkand
3 Cuzco		17 Kabul
4 Bruges	11 Timbuktu	18 Delhi
5 Antwerp	12 Mecca	19 Malacca
6 Mainz	13 Mombasa	20 Beijing
7 Venice	14 Great Zimbabwe	21 Hangzhou
8 Milan		22 Kyoto

The little map shows the world divided into seven regions. The people who lived in a region were linked by customs, traditions, beliefs, or simply by their environment. There were many differences within each region, but the people living there had more in common with one another than with people elsewhere. Each region is shown in a different color. The same colors are used in the headings throughout the book.

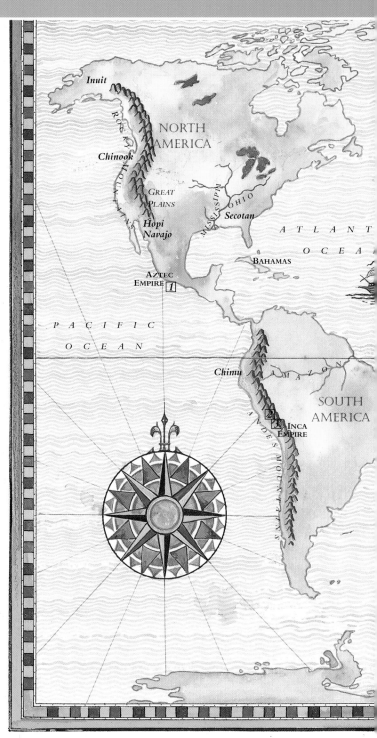

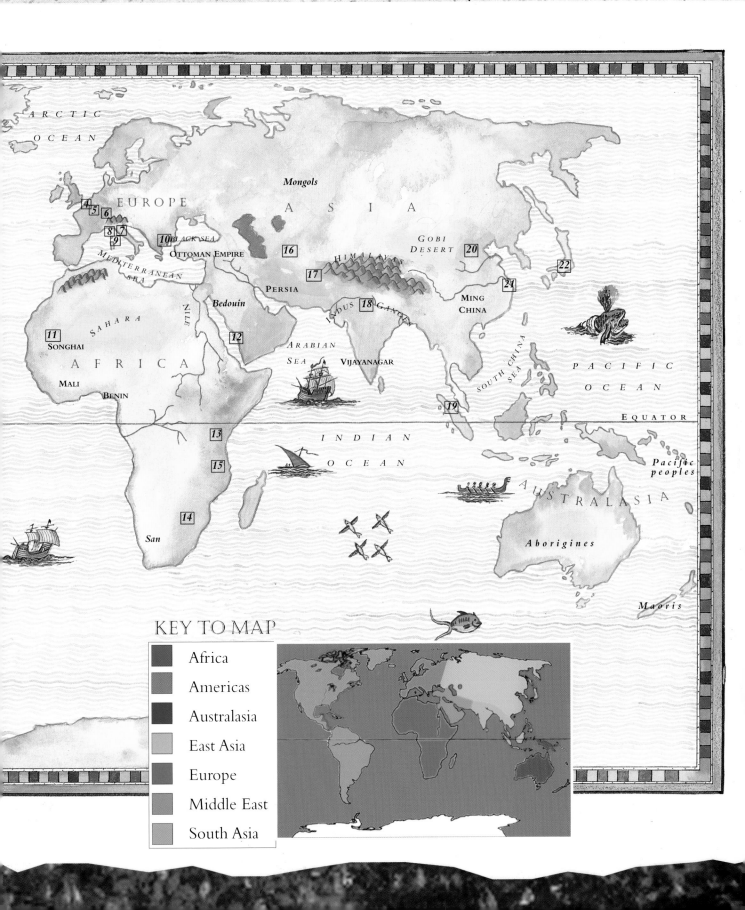

ARCTIC
OCEAN

EUROPE

4
5 6
8 7
9
10 BLACK SEA
Ottoman Empire

MEDITERRANEAN
SEA

ASIA

Mongols

GOBI
DESERT

20

22

16

17

HIMALAYAS

21

NILE

Bedouin

Persia

MING
CHINA

SAHARA

11
Songhai

INDUS

18

GANGES

AFRICA

12

Arabian
Sea

Vijayanagar

Mali

Benin

SOUTH CHINA SEA

PACIFIC
OCEAN

19

EQUATOR

13

INDIAN

OCEAN

15

AUSTRALASIA

Pacific
peoples

14

San

Aborigines

Maoris

KEY TO MAP

	Africa
	Americas
	Australasia
	East Asia
	Europe
	Middle East
	South Asia

TIME LINE

1450   1475

EUROPE

1455–1485 The Wars of the Roses in England.

c.1444–1510 Sandro Botticelli, a famous Italian Renaissance artist.

c.1460 New sailing ships, called carracks are designed for long sea voyages.

c.1490 Ballet dancing created in Italy.

1462–1505 Reign of Ivan the Great of Moscow, who founds the Russian state.

1452 Leonardo da Vinci born.

1453 End of Hundred Years War between England and France.

1475–1564 Michelangelo Buonarroti, an Italian Renaissance sculptor, painter, architect, and poet.

1483–1546 Martin Luther, German leader of the Reformation.

1455 Johannes Gutenberg produces the first printed Bible in Germany.

MIDDLE EAST

1453 Ottoman Turks capture Constantinople and rename it Istanbul.

c.1450 Mocha, in Arabia, becomes the world's main coffee trading port.

1451–1481 Muhammad the Conqueror rules the Ottoman Empire.

AFRICA

c.1464–1591 Songhai Empire rules a large area of West Africa. One of its biggest cities, Timbuktu, becomes a great center of trade, education, and Islamic culture.

1481–1504 Oba Ozolua expands the Benin Empire.

c.1450 The palace-city of Great Zimbabwe, East Africa, begins to be abandoned.

c.1465 Songhai conquers Mali.

c.1486 Portuguese explorers arrive in the city of Benin.

EAST ASIA

c.1467–1477 Onin War between rival Japanese warlords. Civil wars in Japan continue for next 100 years.

1490 Takamoto-Bokuden of the most famous sword ever, born in Japan.

1419–1450 King Sejong rules Korea. Invents a new Korean alphabet, called Hangul. It is still used today.

1473 Shogun Yoshimasa of Japan gives up power. Spends the rest of his life encouraging the arts.

SOUTH ASIA

1469–1539 Guru Nanak, founder of the Sikh faith.

c.1450 Hindu kingdom of Vijayanagar powerful in southern India.

1471 Vietnamese Empire expands southward.

AUSTRALASIA

c.1450 Maori continue to migrate from North Island to South Island of New Zealand.

1450–1550 Migration continues between various islands in the Pacific Ocean.

1500 Chinese sailors may have reached the north coast of Australia by this time and traded with the Aborigines who lived there.

AMERICAS

1440–1468 Moctezuma I expands Aztec Empire.

1438–1471 Emperor Pachacuti expands Inca Empire.

1470 Incas conquer Chimu nation (in present-day northern Peru).

c.1450 Incas build fortress city of Machu Picchu in Andes Mountains.

1492 Columbus sails to America. He thinks he has reached East Asia.

Many of the dates shown in this Time Line are approximate. The letter *c.* stands for the Latin word *circa* and means "about."

1500

1525

1550

1494 Spain and Portugal agree to divide between them all new lands that European explorers reach in America and the Far East.

c.1497–1543 Hans Holbein the Younger, an important Renaissance artist from northern Europe.

1509–1564 John Calvin, French leader of Church reform.

1519 Ferdinand Magellan sets off from Spain to sail around the world.

1519 Leonardo da Vinci dies.

1509-1547 King Henry VIII rules England and Wales.

1520 First state lottery begins in France.

1512–1594 Mapmaker known as Mercator creates a new way to make maps that show the whole world on a flat sheet of paper.

1543 Copernicus publishes a book claiming that the earth travels round the sun. (Later banned by the Church.)

1499 War between Ottoman Turks and Venice, Italy.

1501 Ismail I conquers Persia and declares himself shah (king). His dynasty, the Safavids, rules until 1722.

1509 Istanbul destroyed by earthquake.

1514 War between Turks and Persians.

1516–1517 Ottoman Turks conquer Syria and Arabia.

1520–1566 Suleiman the Magnificent rules the Ottoman Empire.

1526 Turks conquer Hungary.

1505 Portuguese capture the rich trading city of Kilwa on East African coast.

c.1509 Portuguese build forts on the West African coast.

c.1510 First African slaves are transported to the Caribbean.

1517 Ottoman Turks conquer Egypt.

1510–1540 Hausa kingdoms become powerful in West Africa.

1535 Charles V, Holy Roman Emperor, conquers Tunis on North African coast.

1522–1591 Sen-no-Rikyu, the most famous master of the Japanese tea ceremony. He believed that the calm mood the ceremony created was more important than the implements used.

1543 First record of Europeans landing in Japan, shipwrecked there by a storm.

1550 Japanese pirate raids on Chinese coast.

c.1550 Mongols invade northern China.

1498 Portuguese explorer Vasco da Gama sails around the southern tip of Africa and across the Indian Ocean to reach India.

c.1500 Muslim sultans rule Sumatra and Java.

1511 Portuguese explorers arrive in Thailand.

1511 Portuguese traders settle in Malacca (in present-day Malaysia).

1521 Magellan is killed fighting in local war in Philippines.

1526 Babur conquers North India and founds Mogul Empire.

1520 Portuguese explorer Ferdinand Magellan becomes the first European to sail around South America and enter the Pacific Ocean.

1526 Portuguese sailors arrive in Papua New Guinea.

1497 English explorer John Cabot lands in Newfoundland, Canada, and claims the territory for England.

1507 The word *America* is used on a map for the first time, for Italian explorer Amerigo Vespucci, who proved America was a new continent in the West and not part of Asia.

1519 Chocolate sent to Spain from Mexico.

1519–1521 Hernán Cortés conquers Aztec Empire.

1532–1533 Francisco Pizarro conquers Inca Empire.

1550 By now potatoes and tobacco have reached Europe from the Americas.

c.1550 Five Native American nations in Northeast America form the Iroquois Confederacy.

AROUND THE WORLD

For most of Leonardo's lifetime, much of the world was at war. Sometimes wars were fought when powerful kingdoms or city-states tried to conquer their weaker neighbors. Sometimes there were fights between rival religious groups or between princes quarreling over who should be king.

This was also a time when adventurers and explorers, mostly from Spain and Portugal, were beginning to make contact with parts of the world that Europeans had not known about before. They were seeking treasure and trade and hoping to find the quickest way to sail from Europe to rich Asian lands on the other side of the world.

▲ This manuscript illustration shows French and English soldiers fighting during the Hundred Years' War, which lasted from 1337 to 1453. (The French are on the right.) Knights on horseback are wearing heavy metal armor. They are fighting against ordinary soldiers armed with deadly longbows.

A HUNDRED YEARS OF WAR

EUROPE

For many years England and France had been fighting over England's claim to rule parts of France. In 1453, just after Leonardo was born, peace was finally agreed to, and England lost its claim. The war, which became known as the Hundred Years' War, brought death and disaster to ordinary French people. Their farms were destroyed, and their cities were looted by armies, which often ran out of control.

THE WARS OF THE ROSES

Despite the fighting between kingdoms and cities, parts of Europe were growing rich. Many towns such as Bruges, Antwerp, and Venice were great centers of trade. In England there was a successful cloth-making industry. But only two years after France and England had made peace, many parts of the country were caught up in a civil war. Rival nobles struggled over who should rule England, and there were outbreaks of fighting between 1455 and 1485. The fighting became known as the Wars of the Roses, after the red and white rose badges that some of the rival soldiers wore.

THE FALL OF CONSTANTINOPLE

MIDDLE EAST

The Ottoman dynasty was founded around 1300 by a Turkish war-leader called Osman I. At first the Ottoman sultans ruled only a small kingdom in Turkey, but by Leonardo's time their Muslim empire had become the most powerful state in eastern Europe, North Africa, and the Middle East. In 1453 the Ottomans captured Constantinople, a city that had been ruled by Christian emperors for a thousand years. They renamed it Istanbul and made it their capital city. The sultans lived there in splendid palaces, hung with beautiful Middle Eastern silks and carpets.

▼ This wall painting shows Ottoman Turkish troops surrounding the walled city of Constantinople. The last Christian emperor died fighting with his soldiers at the top of the city walls.

RUNNING THE EMPIRE

The Ottoman Empire was run by well-trained slaves. Some were bought from slave traders, and others were captured in war. But the top jobs in the army and the civil service were filled by slaves specially recruited from Christian lands. Officers chose the strongest, most intelligent, and best-looking boys. Some trained as fierce, brilliant soldiers, called janissaries. Others were taught Turkish, Persian, and Arabic (the languages spoken in the empire), law, history, and philosophy. When they qualified, they worked as local governors, tax collectors, and administrators. The cleverest were sent to the capital to become political advisers to the sultan and his court.

▲ The city of Timbuktu grew rich as a center of trade. Merchants traveling by camel across the Sahara stayed in fine houses there. The houses were designed in both African and Arabic styles.

THE OBAS OF BENIN

The kingdom of Benin in western Africa first became powerful around 1400. During Leonardo's lifetime, the obas (kings) of Benin led their armies to conquer new villages and land. They surrounded their capital city, also called Benin, with massive earthworks and huge walls to defend it. The city of Benin was a great center of trade. The obas built new markets and encouraged well-organized groups of craft workers to live and work for them there. Metalwork and cloth from Benin were highly prized, and Benin traders were famous for their business skills. For money, they used beautiful cowrie shells fished from the sea.

EXPLORERS FROM PORTUGAL

During the 1400s explorers from Portugal sailed down the west coast of Africa and reached the city of Benin about 1486. They hoped to find gold, but gold was mined in other African kingdoms, such as Mali and Songhai. So the Portuguese bought slaves from Benin traders instead.

Thousands of miles away, on the East African coast, merchants from Arabia, India, and even China traded with the rich cities of Kilwa and Mombasa. They also made contact with gold miners, cattle keepers, and craft workers who lived in the rich inland kingdom of Zimbabwe.

◀ This brass plaque from Benin, probably made in the 1500s, shows an oba. He is holding two fierce leopards, as a sign of his royal power.

MING RULERS

EAST ASIA

China was ruled by the Ming dynasty during Leonardo's time. In 1368 the first Ming emperor had ended over 100 years of foreign rule by driving Mongol armies from his land. From then on the Ming emperors had three main goals—to rebuild their kingdom's strength and wealth, to encourage Chinese customs and civilization, and to keep all foreign armies and any foreign influence out of their lands.

▼ A typical scene in war-torn Japan. Samurai warriors on horseback lead their armies to surround a rival warlord's castle. This picture was painted later, when much of the fighting was over.

CIVIL WAR

In Japan, as in Europe, there were bitter civil wars that lasted from about 1350 to 1600, as rival warlords, called samurai, struggled for power. Samurai were well-trained and followed a warrior code in which bravery and honor were more important than anything else. They kept their own private armies and lived in fine castles. Samurai who lived on the seacoast led cruel and fearless pirate fleets. Because there was no strong government, the country had many bandit gangs.

In 1543 the first-known Europeans landed in Japan. They were soon followed by traders and by Christian missionaries, but after less than 100 years, the Japanese drove all foreigners away.

INVASION

During the 1400s, India and the nearby lands were divided into several kingdoms, including Delhi in the north, ruled by Muslims, and the Hindu empire of Vijayanagar in the south. There were also many powerful independent princes. In 1526, Babur, a warrior prince from Central Asia, invaded India and conquered the rich city of Delhi and all its lands.

NEW TRADE

In Southeast Asia, merchants traded with travelers from many lands. The first European merchant ships began to arrive in South Asian ports, and the Europeans set up trading posts there. The ships carried valuable goods from the East, such as spices, cloth, and jewels, more quickly and easily than earlier merchants traveling overland.

HUNTING AND TRADING

AUSTRALASIA

The Aborigines of Australia were skillful hunters, fishermen, and trappers. They lived in close-knit family groups. At times when there was plenty of food, families met together to exchange news, sort out disputes, and trade food and goods they had made. People living on the northern coast of Australia traded with sailors from Indonesia and from islands in the Indian Ocean. The Indonesians were in contact with Arabian spice traders and, after 1520, with explorers from Europe, too.

▼ The Portuguese trading post at Malacca, on the southwest coast of the Malay Peninsula. You can see the governor's big house and a Christian church inside the strong walls. Outside the walls are merchant houses, storerooms, and rain-forest trees.

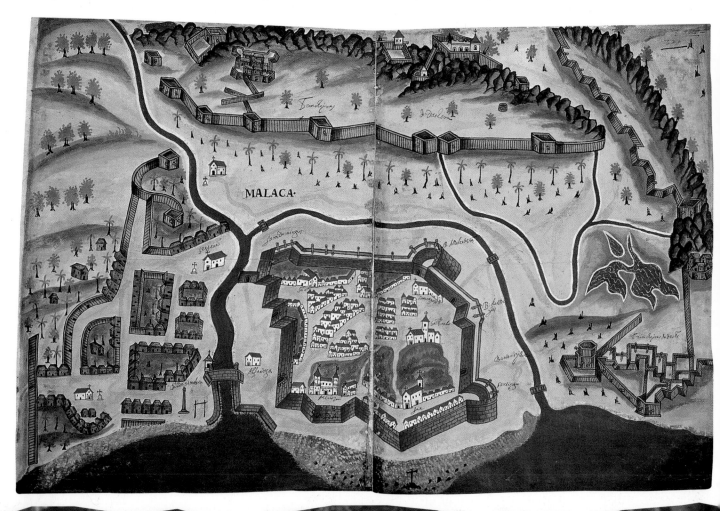

CITIES IN THE NORTH

AMERICAS

North America was home to about 300 Native American groups in Leonardo's time. They all had different lifestyles, from the trading cities along the Mississippi River valley to the Inuit villages in the icy north.

Although Viking traders had reached North America hundreds of years before, people in Leonardo's time did not know this. For them, the first contact between Europe and the Americas was Columbus's journey there in 1492.

THE AZTECS

A warlike people called the Aztecs lived in present-day Mexico and ruled a mighty empire. Conquered peoples paid Aztec rulers tribute— gold dust, cocoa beans, jaguar skins, and precious feathers from tropical birds. The Aztecs called themselves the Mexica. They were skillful builders, farmers, and craft workers. For safety they built their capital city, Tenochtitlán, in the middle of a lake. Almost a quarter of a million people lived there in Leonardo da Vinci's time.

▶ This silver figure was made by a craft worker living in the Inca capital city of Cuzco. It was made for a rich person to give as an offering to the gods.

THE INCAS

The Incas ruled over an empire that stretched more than 2,500 miles along the Pacific coast. The capital city was Cuzco, in present-day Peru. From there, Inca emperors ruled over a well-organized work force. Peasants farmed the rugged mountainsides. Craft workers made magnificent buildings and works of art in precious metals.

The last Inca ruler, Atahualpa, had to defend his lands against Spanish treasure seekers. They were armed with guns that were far more powerful than the Incas' clubs. Thousands of Incas also died of diseases brought by the Europeans. Atahualpa was captured by Spanish soldiers in 1532. Even though his loyal subjects collected an enormous fortune in gold and silver to offer as a ransom, the Spaniards executed him in 1533 and took control of the empire.

◀ In this painting, Aztec warriors are being led by an important noble called an eagle knight. He is wearing a special uniform made out of an eagle's feathered skin. The Aztec armies terrified many nearby peoples, but in 1521 they were defeated by Spanish soldiers led by Hernán Cortés.

FAMOUS RULERS AND LEADERS

The rulers and leaders who lived in Leonardo's time were eager to conquer more land and establish huge empires. But many warlike rulers, such as the Ottoman Sultan Suleiman and the Mogul Emperor Babur, were also great patrons of art and literature. They spent vast amounts of money encouraging artists and craft workers to produce great works. Jewels, portraits, and palaces created a good image and showed how rich and strong the rulers were.

Many rulers were also genuinely interested in art and liked the company of great artists. The Holy Roman Emperor Charles V even made the brilliant Italian painter Titian a nobleman in 1533, because he liked his work so much.

▲ This picture of Charles V was painted by the Italian painter Titian. It shows Charles as a powerful leader. He ruled as Holy Roman Emperor from 1519 to 1556, and collected more land, through diplomacy and war, than any other European ruler before.

LORENZO DE' MEDICI

In Leonardo's time Italy was made up of many city-states. One of the most important was Florence. It was a republic, ruled by the powerful Medici family, who made money from banking. Lorenzo de' Medici ruled Florence from 1469 to 1492. He was famous throughout Europe for his love of the arts. He invited artists, architects, scholars, writers, musicans, and philosophers to eat with him every day, so that he could keep up to date with the latest ideas. He also gave public entertainments for the people of Florence to enjoy. Lorenzo believed that beautiful surroundings would help people live better lives. He worked with other rich citizens to rule the city wisely and well.

▲ King Henry VIII liked music and wrote at least 34 compositions. Here he is shown with his court jester, Will Sommers. Henry is playing the harp.

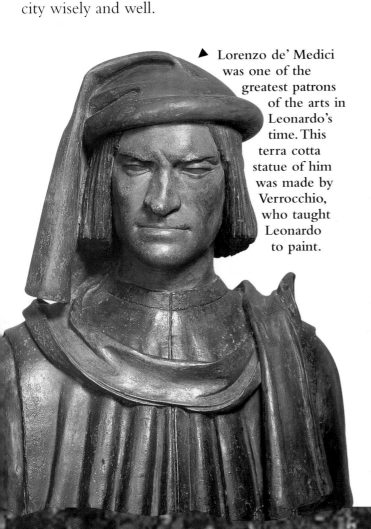

▲ Lorenzo de' Medici was one of the greatest patrons of the arts in Leonardo's time. This terra cotta statue of him was made by Verrocchio, who taught Leonardo to paint.

KING HENRY VIII

King Henry VIII ruled England and Wales from 1509 to 1547. He was praised as a typical Renaissance prince. He was well educated, spoke several languages, was fond of music and art, and was brave on the battlefield. He also enjoyed hunting and tennis—a new sport at the time.

A NEW WIFE AND NEW RELIGION

Henry VIII was interested in religious arguments in Europe (see page 43), and at first supported the Roman Catholic Church. But when the Pope refused to allow him to divorce his wife and marry again, he decided to separate the English Church from the rule of the Pope in Rome. He married Anne Boleyn and set up a new Church of England with himself as its head. Anne Boleyn had a daughter, but no sons, so Henry had her executed and married again. His third wife had a son, who became King Edward VI, but in 1558 Henry and Anne's daughter became a much greater ruler—Elizabeth I of England.

THE CONQUEROR

MIDDLE EAST

Ottoman Sultan Muhammad II, nicknamed the Conqueror, ruled from 1451 to 1481. He became sultan when he was only 19 and led the armies that captured the city of Constantinople. He spent most of his life fighting. By the end of his reign, the Ottoman Empire was larger and stronger than ever before.

THE MAGNIFICENT LAWMAKER

Sultan Suleiman I was born about 1494. He ruled from 1520 to 1566 and was another great Ottoman war leader. His warships controlled the Mediterranean Sea. In Europe he became known as Suleiman the Magnificent, because he spent so much money as a patron of architecture and the arts. In the Ottoman lands he earned the name Suleiman the Lawmaker, because he reformed the Ottoman system of government and passed many new laws.

OZOLUA'S DOWNFALL

AFRICA

Oba Ozolua, who ruled Benin from about 1481 to 1504, expanded his empire by conquering nearby lands belonging to rival peoples. But after many years of war, his soldiers began to feel that Ozolua cared only for his own glory and did not mind how many people died. So they shot him with a poisoned arrow. They did this while Ozolua was having a bath, because it was one of the few times he took his armor off.

FIGHTING FOR POWER

The obas of Benin had many wives. When an oba died, there was often a struggle between the sons of different mothers over who should be the next ruler. After Ozolua's death his son Esigie had to fight to become oba. But Esigie preferred to spend his time peacefully. He encouraged craft workers and promoted trade. He made friends with Portuguese merchants and probably spoke Portuguese.

▶ Queen Idia of Benin, Oba Esigie's mother. The artist has shown her wearing a royal headdress made of coral beads. Esigie gave his mother an important role in ruling the country and built a special palace for her.

◀ Muhammad the Conqueror is shown here, wearing rich royal robes. Artists often painted their rulers holding a rose to show that they were not just warriors, but men of taste who enjoyed beauty, too.

MONGOLS AND THE MING

EAST ASIA

In the years before Leonardo was born, China was ruled by a wise and powerful Ming emperor called Yonglo. But he died in 1424, and the emperors of the Ming Dynasty who ruled after him were much less successful. One, called Cheng Tung, set off north in 1449 to fight the Mongols. They captured him, and the government had to pay a lot of money before he was set free. After this the Mongols were angry at being attacked and invaded China. At the same time, pirate leaders who sailed in the South China Sea took advantage of these fights to attack Chinese merchant ships. For many years after Cheng Tung's adventure, Chinese rulers had to spend most of their time trying to defend their lands.

CIVIL WAR

In Japan, although there was an emperor, the country was really ruled by a warrior leader, called a shogun. One family, the Ashikaga, had ruled for more than 100 years, but in 1467 they fought among themselves over who should be the next shogun. This led to a war that almost destroyed the emperor's royal city of Kyoto. In 1473 the ruling shogun, called Yoshimasa, retired to his palace on the outskirts of Kyoto and spent his time with Japan's best artists, poets, and musicians. Other warlord families battled on for the title of shogun. The fighting was finally ended by General Oda Nobunaga.

▲ Chinese rulers lived in this palace in Beijing. In the 1400s, the old mud and straw walls were replaced with solid stone, and many beautiful halls and temples were built. The palace was called the Forbidden City, because ordinary people were not allowed in.

▼ General Oda Nobunaga, who lived from 1534 to 1582, helped to end the long years of civil war in Japan. He forced most of the warrior leaders to obey his commands. He is shown here looking very fierce in full armor.

BABUR'S CONQUESTS

SOUTH ASIA

Babur was born in Central Asia, in 1483, and founded a mighty empire in India. When he was only 14 years old he led a successful raid on the rich city of Samarkand, and in 1504, when he was 21, he captured the important fortress of Kabul, in present-day Afghanistan. By 1526 he had conquered the sultanate of Delhi. He died in 1530, by which time he controlled most of northern India.

Babur was brave and ruthless—his name means tiger. But he could also be thoughtful and sensitive. He loved books, pictures, poetry, and jewels. He was descended from two great Mongol warlords called Timur and Genghis Khan. The dynasty he founded became known as Mogul, which meant Mongol in Persian, the language spoken by many scholars in India.

▲ This painting, made in 1528, shows the first Mogul emperor, Babur, in a garden with his courtiers. Babur collected many rare and beautiful plants.

ELDERS AND WAR LEADERS

AUSTRALASIA

We do not know the names of any leaders among the Aborigines of Australia or of the Maori in New Zealand. But traditions and stories tell us a little about what their duties may have been. Family groups were guided by elders. These were older people who passed on their experience and kept younger people under control. Maori chiefs were war leaders. They had to be ready to avenge an insult, to defend their homes and families, or to win honor by killing their enemies on surprise raids.

◄ Maori chiefs had to defend their villages and farms from enemy warrior bands. This picture was painted after Leonardo's time, but shows clothes and weapons that had changed little since then.

BUILDING THE INCA EMPIRE

The Inca ruler Pachacuti Yupanqui behaved like many other leaders in Leonardo's time. He planned and led a series of wars to make his empire bigger and conquered many nearby lands. But to the Inca people, Pachacuti was more than just a brilliant battle commander. They believed he was the son of the Sun and had absolute power. To keep their god-like blood pure, Inca kings only married other family members, although many had extra wives as well.

▼ Moctezuma II ruled the Aztec Empire from 1502 to 1520. This picture of him is from an Aztec book called a codex. He is shown here being crowned.

▲ Pachacuti ruled the Inca empire from 1438 to 1471. He was a brilliant leader and organizer. There were no paintings of Inca rulers made at the time, and this later picture was painted by a European about 1750. It is based on traditional stories about Pachacuti and on travelers' descriptions of Inca clothes and jewels.

MOCTEZUMA II

Early Aztec rulers were bold warriors, but Moctezuma II, who came to power in 1502, was more interested in religion. When Spanish conquerers landed in Mexico in 1519, he thought they were gods and refused to fight. The Spaniards put him in prison. Other Aztec leaders tried to drive the Spaniards out of their lands, but they failed. Moctezuma died mysteriously during the fighting, in 1520. No one knows whether he was killed by the Spaniards or by his own people who were angry because he wouldn't fight.

HOW PEOPLE LIVED

▲ This Italian painting shows peasant men and women busy harvesting wheat. Inside the city wall in the foreground of the picture, well-dressed nobles look on.

Leonardo lived in Florence, one of the richest cities in Europe. Its rulers and citizens were rich enough to pay for fine buildings and beautiful works of art, and also for programs to provide food and money for poor people who came to their city in search of help.

All around the world there were great differences in living standards between the rich and the poor. Some groups, like the Incas in South America, set up welfare programs. Some rulers, like the kings of England and France, tried to solve the problem of homeless beggars by passing strict laws. Religious leaders from many faiths taught that charity was a holy duty. But often people who were too ill to work, or who had no money, had to rely on their families and friends, or else starve.

▲ This manuscript illustration shows sheep being sheared. Many farmers in northern Europe grew rich by keeping flocks of sheep and selling their wool.

TOWN LIFE

EUROPE

Life in a European town could be comfortable for rich people, such as nobles, lawyers, top churchmen, successful merchants, and craft workers. They could afford a large house on a quiet street, good food from the markets, and servants to look after them. Poor people lived in overcrowded homes. The back streets were often full of dirt and disease.

POVERTY AND PROBLEMS

Most people in Europe lived in the countryside. They worked as farm laborers or as servants in big houses. Their lives became even harder after around 1500. The population began to grow, so there was less food to go around, and it became more expensive. At the same time wages fell, because there were lots of people looking for work and not enough jobs. In England, Belgium, and Germany, there were riots. The poorest people were often starving. Some people were driven to stealing money, goods, or even food. Governments reacted by passing harsh new laws.

FARMS AND TOWNS

MIDDLE EAST

In the Middle Eastern countryside, farmers lived in small villages. They raised sheep and goats and planted orchards of apricots, almonds, and olives. Where soils were rich and there was a good water supply, they grew wheat, barley, grapes, figs, and melons. Oxen were used to pull plows, and donkeys carried loads up steep mountain tracks.

Craft workers and merchants lived in busy trading towns, where there were huge covered markets, called souks. Visitors could buy everyday clothes and household items or the most expensive silks, jewels, and perfumes in the world.

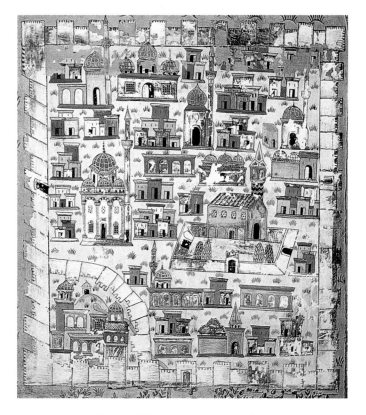

▲ A town in Turkey. Towns in the Middle East were well planned, with schools, hospitals, and travelers' lodges. In the picture you can see six mosques, with their domed roofs and minarets. In the left foreground of the picture is the governor's palace.

DESERT TRADE

MIDDLE EAST

In Middle Eastern desert
lands, people kept camels for transportation and
to provide meat and milk. Rich, sticky fruit grew
on wild date palms at oases created by natural
springs. Frankincense and myrrh trees were also
grown for their valuable, sweet-smelling gum.
The Arabian people, called Bedouins, followed
an ancient nomadic lifestyle. They lived in tents
made from woven goats' hair and earned money
by breeding camels, horses, and hunting dogs.
They also led trains of camels loaded with
precious spices, gold, gemstones, and pearls
across the deserts to trade at busy seaports.

TOWNS AND VILLAGES

AFRICA

There were many rich and thriving towns in
Africa, including Timbuktu and Benin. But most
people in Africa made their living from the land.
In the tropical rain forests of West and Central
Africa, farmers cleared fields to grow vegetables
such as yams and plantains. In drier, cooler
regions, such as Zimbabwe, people grew crops
of millet and sorghum, which they pounded
and mixed with boiled water to make a thick,
soft food.

Women usually sowed and harvested the crops,
cooked, and fetched water from rivers or wells. It
was hard and tiring work, especially as they had
to look after their children and clean their houses
as well. In the driest regions of Africa, food crops
would not grow, so cattle were the main source
of food. Cattle were usually looked after by men.

▲ Many edible plants,
such as mangoes and plantains,
grew wild in West Africa. This bronze
plaque from Benin shows a servant
climbing a tree to gather fruit.

NOMADIC LIFE

In nomadic communities, such as the San in
southern Africa, men herded cattle and hunted.
They tracked or trapped wild animals and birds
and killed them with spears, or bows and arrows,
sometimes tipped with poison. Women gathered
fruits, roots, and wild honey for food.

► People had herded cattle for thousands
of years in many parts of Africa, and
little had changed by Leonardo's time.
This ancient rock painting shows African
herders and their cattle.

RICE TAXES IN JAPAN

EAST ASIA

Rice was the staple food for most people living in East Asia. Rice was so important that in Japan it was used to measure a nobleman's wealth. Peasants often paid their taxes to landowners in rice. This could be up to half the crop, and peasants sometimes rioted in protest.

Growing rice was exhausting and skillful work. Peasants had to stand ankle-deep in water in flooded fields to plant the rice seedlings. They had to control very carefully how much water flowed into the fields to be sure of a successful crop. When the rice was ripe, the fields were drained, and the long rice stalks cut. They were carted to the farmyard to be dried and threshed.

▼ In the picture, Japanese women are beating bunches of rice against straw matting to separate the grains of rice from the stalks. Behind them men are polishing the grains by turning them in a big mill.

HOUSEBOATS AND PEARL FISHING

The Chinese population grew substantially between 1400 and 1550. This meant more demand for food and clothing. Peasants cleared new land, planned new irrigation projects, and planted new crops, such as cotton. Along the coast and on China's rivers and canals, many families lived on boats. They made money from fishing, ferrying travelers, or transporting heavy loads. Sometimes children were kidnapped by merchants and forced to work as divers, gathering pearl oysters from the ocean floor. Many drowned.

BIG CITIES

In China there were many large cities and towns, such as Hangzhou and Beijing, where people earned a living from making craft goods and from trade. In Japan the city of Kyoto was the center of government. Like all large towns it had theaters, restaurants, and bath houses, where people could relax and be entertained.

VILLAGES AND TRADE

Most people in India lived in villages. In the dry Northwest, farmers grew crops such as wheat and chickpeas and lived in houses made of sun-baked mud brick. In the hot, rainy South, they grew rice, pepper, spices, mangoes, and coconuts. Their houses had bamboo walls with roofs made of palm-leaf thatch.

Indian craft workers made jewelry, glassware, metalwork, and leather goods. Indian cloth had been famous in Europe and the Middle East since Roman times. In 1498, Vasco da Gama was the first European to sail around southern Africa to reach India's west-coast trading ports. Others soon followed, and trade with Europe increased.

HUNTERS AND GATHERERS

Over thousands of years the Aborigines of Australia had learned to survive in a harsh environment. People sometimes ate kangaroos, emu, shellfish, turtles, roasted moths, possums, and birds' eggs. But mostly they ate plants, such as grass seeds, berries, and yams. Women also dug up lizards and insect grubs for food. Most people were nomads. They moved from camp to camp, reaching each one when the local food supply of birds, fish, insects, and plants was at its best.

MAORI FORTS AND FARMS

Many of the Maori people of New Zealand were farmers. They lived in villages, called pa, which were defended against enemies by wooden fences or stone walls. On the warm North Island, the Maori grew kumara, an orange-fleshed sweet potato. On the South Island, where it is colder and wetter, people fished and trapped seabirds. Everywhere Maori people gathered bracken roots, dried them, ground them up, and cooked them with water to make a sticky paste.

▼ Aborigine hunters used spears and boomerangs (throwing sticks) to catch many different wild animals for food. They were experts at following tracks and setting traps. This painting, made by a European artist in 1817, shows ancient hunting techniques of the Aborigines. The hunters are hiding behind trees and bushes ready to attack some kangaroos.

LIVING WITH THE ENVIRONMENT

AMERICAS

The landscape and the climate of North America range from snowy mountains to tropical swamps, and from rocky desert canyons to wide, windswept prairies. So the Native American peoples who lived there had very different lifestyles. Some, like the Chinook on the Northwest Coast, lived in wooden houses and caught fish. Others, like the Hopi in the Southwest, lived in apartment blocks made of sun-dried bricks called adobe. They grew crops on irrigated lands. The now extinct Secotan lived in woodlands along the East Coast. They hunted deer, caught fish, and grew corn.

THE CENTER OF THE EMPIRE

The Aztec capital city of Tenochtitlán was surrounded by floating gardens called chinampas, made of woven branches and mud from the lake bottom. Here farmers grew crops such as avocados, tomatoes, peppers, and chillies. The Aztecs' staple food was corn, which they made into crispy pancakes and ate with spicy vegetable stew. People could also buy delicacies at the city market, such as cocoa powder, which they used to make a drink called "chocolatl."

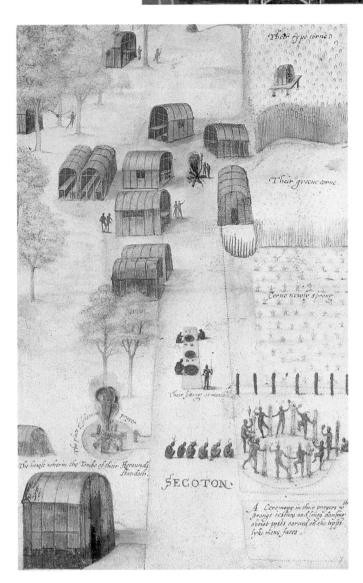

▲ This picture was painted by an English traveler about 1584. It shows a village built by the Secotan people. The houses are built of wood, with roofs made of waterproof tree bark and woven straw.

◀ A silver statue of a llama made by an Inca craft worker in Peru

INCA LIFESTYLE

Most Inca people lived in steep mountain valleys, or on high windswept plains, where only a few crops, such as potatoes, could grow. Farmers kept herds of llamas and alpacas. Women wove llama hair into warm cloaks and blankets. The Incas had no wheeled transportation, so they also used llamas to carry heavy loads up steep mountain tracks.

DISCOVERY AND INVENTION

Leonardo lived at a time when European scientists were challenging many of the teachings they had learned from the Church and at universities. They wanted to observe the world, make experiments, and find out things for themselves. They made many important discoveries, especially in astronomy and anatomy.

One of the most important inventions during this time was the printing press. The invention of printing meant that more people could read about new ideas more quickly than before. Soon news of inventions and discoveries, including information about life outside Europe, was beginning to spread through many lands. More people were beginning to explore the world in the hope of making money from trade and treasure.

◄ Printing workshops were set up in many European cities. Printers arranged individual letters, made of metal or wood, to make up words on a page. At first they printed copies of the Bible and other religious writings. But by the 1500s they were also printing books on travel and science, maps, diaries, and plays.

THE PRINTING PRESS

EUROPE

The first large-scale printing workshop in Europe was set up by Johann Gutenberg, in the German city of Mainz, about 1450. It held six new printing presses with movable type. Printing was not a European invention. The Chinese had discovered how to do it hundreds of years before. But because their language has more than 3,000 characters, Chinese scholars found it quicker to copy out books by hand.

THE GREAT EXPLORERS

Christopher Columbus was not the the first person to think the world was round. But he was the first to try and reach India and the Far East by sailing west from Europe, across the uncharted Atlantic Ocean. The king and queen of Spain gave him money for the journey, because they wanted to find a new trade route for their Spanish ships. Columbus crossed the Atlantic in 1492. He did not realize that he had, in fact, landed in the Americas, and not in India.

NEW SCIENCE

In 1543 a Polish astronomer called Nicolaus Copernicus published a book saying that the earth moved around the sun. Before this, people thought that the earth was at the center of the universe. Also in 1543 a Belgian doctor called Vesalius published the first European book with pictures of the human body and diagrams of how bones and muscles work.

AROUND THE WORLD

The first voyage around the world was planned by a Portuguese navigator called Ferdinand Magellan. He set off from Spain in 1519 with five ships and about 237 men. Although he was killed in the Philippines, the voyage was completed by Captain Sebastian del Cano. He arrived home in 1522, after three years at sea, with only one ship and 17 members of the original crew alive.

◀ In the 1400s and 1500s, bigger, stronger ships were built to carry explorers on long voyages. This ship has big square sails to catch the wind. It is armed with cannons to fight off pirates.

▼ A diagram showing Copernicus's new ideas. The sun (with a face) is in the center, with the planets around it. Earth is shown as a blue and green globe above the sun.

AN IMPORTANT DRINK

MIDDLE EAST

Coffee trees first grew naturally in northeastern Africa. But in the 1400s, Arab traders brought coffee seedlings from Ethiopia to start coffee plantations in Arabia. The habit of drinking coffee became very fashionable. It spread throughout the Muslim world, carried home by travelers who had made a pilgrimage to the holy city of Mecca. Over the centuries that followed, coffee-drinking has spread worldwide. Coffee is now one of the most important products in international trade.

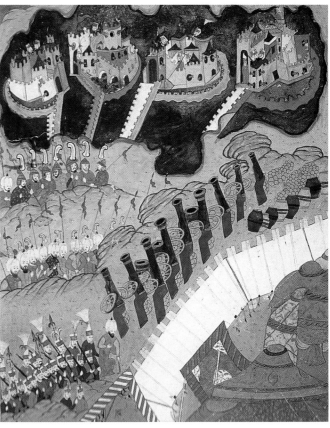

▲ Cannons changed warfare and made traditional city defenses almost useless. This picture shows an Ottoman army with its cannons, cannonballs, and gunpowder barrels.

BIG GUNS

Guns and cannons were used more and more in Europe and the Middle East in Leonardo's time, and the Ottomans made some of the best cannons in the world. The largest were made of bronze and could fire a heavy cannon ball at targets more than a mile away. They could be up to 20 feet long, and cast in two pieces. Sultan Muhammad II used cannons like these to smash the walls of Constantinople, which had survived all other attacks for more than 1,000 years.

◀ This Turkish miniature shows guests drinking coffee at a banquet. Servants are busy with coffee cups on the right, toward the back. Behind them the host entertains his most important guests.

BUILDING IN A HOT, WET CLIMATE

In West Africa, builders had to cope with a hot climate and heavy rains. The local building materials were sun-baked mud, used to make the walls, and palm-leaf thatch, for the roof. To keep the walls from being washed away in the rain, the leaf roof hung over the edges. People built rooms around an open courtyard so that only a small roof was needed on each side. If they had built square houses with a wide single roof, the leaves would have soaked up too much water and collapsed.

DRY-STONE WALLS

In the rocky uplands of East Africa, people used a technique called dry-stone walling. Small blocks of a hard stone called granite were cut with sharp iron tools, and then arranged in decorative patterns. Only skillful shaping and laying held the blocks in place. The builders did not use cement.

DANGEROUS EXPERIMENTS

Before Leonardo's time, Chinese emperors had encouraged great inventors and explorers. Chinese porcelain, explosives, paper, and silk were famous in many lands. Chinese sailors may even have explored as far as Australia. After about 1430, expeditions stopped, and scientists made few discoveries for 100 years. But some inventors still tried out new ideas. People told how scientist Wu Han in 1500 used gunpowder to launch a rocket that would let him fly through the air. It exploded and he was killed.

SAMURAI ARMOR

In Japan many years of war led to changes in samurai armor. Important warriors still wore splendid armor at court, but on the battlefield they needed something more practical. Usually they fought on foot with swords, so they needed armor that allowed them to move easily. During the late 1400s, a lightweight armor was developed, made of little metal plates sewn onto cloth. Once guns began to be used in Japan, about 1543, inventors designed bullet-resistant armor made of hinged iron plates.

▶ Samurai armor was often destroyed in battle, so little survives. But high-ranking warriors kept armor like this, to wear at important ceremonies. It was made of leather and flexible iron plates. The face was shielded by a fierce iron mask. It was much heavier than battle armor.

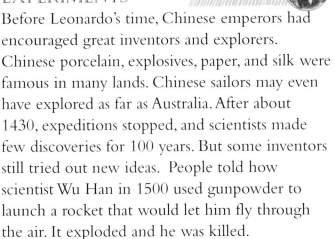

GUNS AND SIEGE WARFARE

When the Mogul leader Babur invaded India and founded an empire, his soldiers carried cannons and hand-held guns with them. They also rode on horseback, in the traditional Mongol way. These horses and guns gave Babur's soldiers a great advantage over the local Indian troops. The Indian armies fought on foot, and their weapons were bows and arrows, spears, and swords. Although they also had war elephants, which usually terrified enemy foot soldiers, Babur's soldiers on their light, nimble horses simply galloped out of the elephants' way.

KNOWING THE SEA

The Pacific peoples were skilled boatbuilders and expert navigators. They used the sun and moon, clouds, currents, and the flight of sea birds to help them steer. They made maps of the ocean, using sticks to mark fast currents and shells and stones to mark islands.

FISHING SKILLS

Aborigine fishermen developed simple but effective techniques to help them work. They used fishing spears tipped with lots of small points (like a very sharp comb) so that a fish could not slip off. They also lit small fires on board their canoes. At dusk the smoke kept biting insects away, and at night the light attracted the fish toward them.

NEW FOODS

When European explorers arrived in America, they found vegetables and spices unknown to the rest of the world. Farmers in America had discovered how to grow crops of corn, potatoes, tomatoes, cocoa, chillies, kidney beans, and sweet peppers. These plants all first arrived in Europe in the 1500s, along with sunflowers, pineapples, and turkeys. Corn was also introduced into Africa and China. Hot, spicy chillies soon became an important ingredient in food in India and nearby lands.

◀ When Babur attacked Indian towns, he used new technology, which you can see in this picture. His soldiers built zigzag walls to hide the cannons, and wood and leather screens for soldiers to hide behind. They dug covered trenches, called sabats, so that soldiers could creep close to enemy walls without being shot at by their enemies high above. Bulls are pulling more cannons up the hill.

MEDICINES

Doctors in the Americas developed their own medical treatments. They made up soothing mixtures of local herbs and used tobacco as a medicine. The Aztecs of central Mexico used chillies as a painkiller and an antiseptic. They also gave people sweat-baths, where patients sat in a hot, steamy hut, like a sauna.

Inca doctors learned how to "trepan" or cut holes in a patient's skull, to relieve pressure on the brain from head injuries. The Incas may also have been the first people in the world to carry out blood transfusions. Because most Incas shared the same blood type, there were few problems finding matching donors.

INCA BUILDINGS

The Inca city of Cuzco was built in the Andes Mountains. Because Cuzco is so high above sea level, few trees grow there, and everything, from huge temples and palaces to peasant huts, had to be built of stone. There were also many earthquakes, so Inca stonemasons developed earthquake-proof buildings. They cut the stone into massive blocks and smoothed the edges using stone tools. Then they fit the blocks tightly together like a giant jigsaw puzzle to build the walls. They did not use mortar. When there was an earthquake, all the stones jumped and shifted a little, and then settled back into place. The roofs of the buildings were made of dried mountain grass.

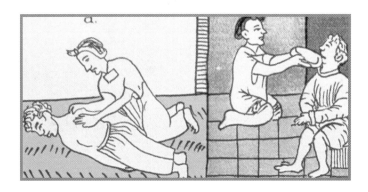

▲ The Aztecs kept notes of medical treatments. This picture from an Aztec book called a codex shows a nurse massaging a patient and a doctor giving some medicine.

▼ The ruins of Machu Picchu, an Inca city high in the Andes Mountains. The straw roofs have gone, but the stone walls have survived about 500 years and many earthquakes.

THE CREATIVE WORLD

During Leonardo's lifetime, people all over the world began to be more aware of works of art from distant lands. More people were traveling farther than before, and explorers and traders took home exotic goods of all kinds. When the Spanish explorer Cortés returned from Mexico, he presented Emperor Charles V with a magnificent Aztec headdress, made of precious bird feathers. European artists often painted luxury objects, such as carpets from the Middle East, in their pictures to create rich and impressive backgrounds.

Indian and Turkish artists began to copy beautiful miniature paintings from Persia. Skilled craft workers in Benin soon began to include figures of Portuguese explorers among the bronze portrait sculptures they made.

▶ This famous statue, called the *Pietà*, was carved by an Italian artist called Michelangelo Buonarroti. It shows the Virgin Mary cradling the dead Jesus Christ. Michelangelo was a skillful sculptor and painter. He mixed Renaissance ideas of human beauty with traditional Christian beliefs.

THE RENAISSANCE

EUROPE

In the 1400s and 1500s, European painters and sculptors began to work in a new style. It was more lifelike and more dramatic than art had ever been before. It also showed human feelings in a new, direct way. People called this new style a "renaissance" of art. (*Renaissance* is a French word meaning "rebirth.") These new ideas and styles spread quickly from Italy, where they began, to the rest of Europe.

RENAISSANCE IDEAS

Renaissance artists and scholars studied ancient Greek and Roman books. From their studies they developed a new way of thinking called humanism. The humanists emphasized the ideas, achievements, and problems of humans in this life, rather than in the world hereafter. They tried to show these beliefs in their work.

▶ Sandro Botticelli was another Renaissance artist, who lived and worked in Florence. He often copied ancient Greek and Roman designs. This is a detail from one of his paintings, *Primavera* (Allegory of Spring). It shows a maiden generally identified with spring.

▲ Hans Holbein was a German painter who spent many years working in England. He painted this picture, called *The Ambassadors*, for King Henry VIII. The men are shown in a lifelike way. The globes, books, and musical instruments show that they were interested in Renaissance arts, science, and ideas.

ART AND NATURE

Two things helped Renaissance artists create a new style. First they studied ancient Greek and Roman paintings and sculptures and learned how to copy their lifelike designs. They also copied their buildings and built churches and palaces to look like Greek and Roman temples. Second, like Leonardo, they studied nature carefully. They tried to show human bodies, plants, and animals in as real a way as possible.

Some artists explored the way our eyes look at things and invented a new painting technique called perspective. This allowed painters to show space and distance inside a picture, even though the painting itself was flat.

OTTOMAN ART

MIDDLE EAST

Sultan Suleiman (see page 20), wore glittering jewels and beautiful clothes. His palace in Istanbul was filled with the best glassware and metalwork that the artists and craft workers of his empire could supply. The palace walls had panels of tiles glazed in bright colors and complicated patterns. The walls were also hung with the finest carpets. The palace gardens were carefully designed and full of sweet-smelling roses and carnations.

▼ This Persian miniature shows a scholar and his pupils. The Ottomans and Indians admired Persian designs, and students often traveled to Persia to study with top artists.

▲ The gardens of Sultan Suleiman's palace. In this Turkish miniature, painted in 1524, you can see courtiers strolling around the grounds, sheltering in a tower, and admiring the rare trees and flowers.

BOOKS AND MINIATURES

The Ottomans gave large sums of money to pay for mosques and tombs. They also encouraged artists to make beautiful books, written in decorative handwriting called calligraphy. The books were bound with leather and studded with precious jewels. Like their neighbors the Persians, the Ottomans admired and collected miniatures. These were detailed little paintings in bright colors. They often showed scenes from traditional stories or of life at the royal court.

AFRICAN BRONZES AND CARVINGS

AFRICA

By Leonardo's time, Benin craft workers had perfected a technique of making beautiful, realistic statues from bronze or brass. They also made bronze plaques, which showed scenes from traditional stories and historic events and recorded important ceremonies. They were used to decorate the walls and gateways of palaces belonging to the oba and to powerful chiefs.

African craft workers also created many brightly colored textiles, woven from wool and cotton. They made masks and sculptures carved from local materials.

MING CHINA

EAST ASIA

Chinese merchants had sold fine china, called porcelain, to Europeans for many years. In Leonardo's time craft workers at the emperor's factory developed a new way of working that allowed them to add bright touches of color to the glaze after it had been fired. Some of the finest Ming porcelain was made for the emperor's court. But most was specially designed to sell in Africa, the Middle East, and Europe, to earn money for China abroad.

▶ West African craft workers made many beautiful objects from precious ivory and tropical woods. This ivory mask was used by the obas of Benin during religious ceremonies. It was worn hanging from a belt.

POEMS AND MANUSCRIPTS

SOUTH ASIA

In India the new Mogul emperors were eager to encourage the arts. Babur, the Mogul conqueror, was a poet. He was also a collector of fine books and manuscripts. Sometimes pictures of birds and flowers were pasted into albums to decorate the text. The palace library held thousands of volumes and was one of the largest in the world.

Babur also liked beautiful surroundings. He employed teams of workers and architects to design flowery meadows and cool, shady gardens with ponds and fountains, where he could relax in the heat of the Indian summer, admire delicate flowers, and eat delicious fruits.

▶ By the 1400s one of the most famous styles of Ming porcelain was blue-and-white china, patterned with plants, flowers, animals, or scenes with people. This vase shows Chinese people at a feast in a garden.

▲ The ruins of Vittala Temple, from the Vijayanagar Empire. It was designed to look like the sun god's chariot.

THE CITY OF VIJAYANAGAR

SOUTH ASIA

In southern India the Hindu kings who ruled the Vijayanagar Empire paid for beautiful palaces and temples to be built. Visitors said the city of Vijayanagar was spectacular. It covered nine square miles and had lakes, canals, fruit gardens, and seven encircling city walls. The king's palace was decorated with carvings of roses and lotus flowers.

MUSIC AND FESTIVALS

AUSTRALASIA

Music was an important part of life for many people around the world. The Aborigines of Australia held special festivals of music and dancing. They sang songs and told stories that had been passed on by word of mouth for thousands of years. They danced to the music of the didgeridoo, a hollow wooden tube that was blown to produce a deep humming sound.

Maori craft workers in New Zealand carved flutes and whistles from wood or bone. They made wooden gongs and trumpets out of conch shells. They also carved detailed patterns in wood to decorate houses, gateways, and canoes.

◄ Carved wooden panels like this one were used to decorate Maori chiefs' houses. This is from the top section of a wooden door frame.

BODY PAINTING AND OTHER ART

AMERICAS

In North America there were many different kinds of art. People made totem poles, leatherwork, and pottery objects. Many people painted their bodies with detailed patterns. They made paints from plants and crushed earth. The patterns were a sign of adulthood and also showed that the wearer belonged to a particular group in society.

Often art had a religious purpose. The Navajo and Hopi people created beautiful pictures out of sand, showing the spirits of earth and sky. These were made as part of a ritual to heal sick people. When the ritual was over, the painting was destroyed.

▶ A mask made of a thin sheet of gold, hammered into a face shape. Masks like this were made in several parts of the Inca empire, especially by the Chimu people. They were often used to cover the faces of dead people.

INCA CRAFT WORKERS

In South America the Inca emperors employed craft workers to weave cloth, mold pottery, and make delicate jewelry out of gold and precious stones. Men and women wore jeweled headbands, earrings, nose studs, and chest ornaments. In Cuzco, the Inca capital city, the biggest temple had a sacred garden full of lifesize animals and food plants made of real gold.

Inca metalworkers had an honored place in the community. Their sons were trained to work with them from a very early age, because it took many years to learn their skills.

▲ This Native American chief was painted in 1585 by John White, one of the first European artists to travel to America. The chief has decorated his body with purple patterns.

INCA MUMMIES

The Incas and other South American peoples believed that silver was the tears of the moon and gold was the sweat of the sun. They also believed that gold had magical qualities. People used it to make masks to cover the faces of dead emperors, before they were made into mummies and entombed. Inca mummies were dressed in rich robes and wrapped in fine-woven cloth. On festival days, people took the mummies from their tombs and carried them through the streets.

BELIEFS AND IDEAS

In Leonardo's time almost everyone in the world believed in some kind of religion. In many lands, laws, scholarship, and education were all based on religious ideas. The biggest, most beautiful buildings were designed for religious use, and all year round there were rituals and festivals that made men, women, and children feel at peace. Religion was also closely linked to politics. In many countries, people of the same faith quarreled and even fought one another over their different religious opinions.

▶ Martin Luther preaching to people who shared his wish for a reformed Church. Preaching was an important way to spread new ideas. This is a detail of a picture painted on strips of wood.

THE REFORMATION

EUROPE

There were many quarrels about religion in Leonardo's time. Almost everyone in Europe followed the Christian faith, and in western Europe people belonged to the Roman Catholic Church. It was rich and powerful, and its leader, the Pope, played an important part in politics. But religious reformers complained that the Church was corrupt and that priests were lazy. They demanded the freedom to worship God in a new way. Reformers wanted to hold church services and read the Bible in their own languages, instead of in Latin, so that people could understand more about their faith.

In the 1500s the reformers set up new churches of their own, led by such men as Martin Luther in Germany and John Calvin in Switzerland. They became known as Protestants, because of their complaints and protests about the Roman Catholic faith.

SPIRIT MASKS

AFRICA

By Leonardo's time many nations in North Africa had been converted to Islam. Elsewhere Africans kept their own ancient beliefs. They believed in one god, who had made the world, and in other lesser gods and spirits.

Most people believed that dead ancestors had the power to help or harm them. Ancestors' bones, or carved masks representing ancestor's spirits, were sometimes kept in a special house in the village. On festival days the masks were carried through streets and fields by men who were members of secret societies, based on family groups or certain trades. Women belonged to secret societies, too. Often, they trained their members in healing skills.

FAITH OF ISLAM

MIDDLE EAST

People in the Middle East followed the faith of Islam. But the two most powerful ruling dynasties, the Ottomans and the Safavids (in Persia) belonged to different branches of the faith. They disagreed over who should lead the Muslim community. Religious disagreement mixed with political rivalry and caused many years of fighting between them.

▲When the Ottomans conquered Constantinople in 1453, they turned its famous Christian church, called Saint Sophia, into a mosque.

RELIGIOUS TOLERANCE

The Ottomans were tolerant toward people of other faiths living in their empire so long as they obeyed Ottoman laws. Ottoman governors worked with Christian leaders to set up a system of local government, which collected taxes and kept law and order in conquered lands.

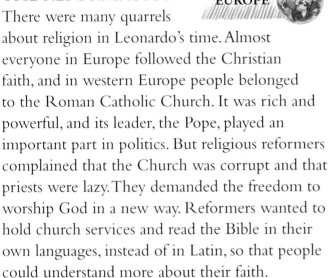

SHINTOISM

In Japan most people followed the ancient Shinto faith. They worshiped many spirits, including gods and goddesses, the souls of past warriors, emperors and famous scholars; their family ancestors; and the spirits who lived in mountains, rocks, and trees. People visited Shinto shrines to ask these divine beings to protect them. Priests who lived at the shrines had powers to bless worshipers. Sometimes they also told people their fortunes.

ZEN BUDDHISM

A new branch of Buddhism had been introduced to Japan from China around 1200. It was called Zen. By Leonardo's time it had become very popular. Zen beliefs and Shinto traditions mixed to form a new set of beliefs, which stressed honor, duty, and respect for national leaders.

▼ Japanese Zen Buddhists made stone gardens like this one, where people could meditate. They believed this would help people think clearly and behave well.

A NEW FAITH

People in India followed different faiths. Most were Hindus, but there were also Muslims, Buddhists, Parsees, and Jains. In Leonardo's time a new religion grew up in India: the Sikh faith. It was founded by Guru Nanak, who was born in northwestern India in 1469. As a young man he traveled around the country, urging people to think about God by singing religious songs.

Nanak became known as Guru, which means "holy teacher." His words were respected by Hindus and Muslims, but soon after Guru Nanak's death, his followers broke away from other religious groups and began to worship in their own way, as Sikhs.

ISLAM IN ASIA

Elsewhere in South Asia, on the islands of present-day Malaysia and Indonesia, many people were being converted to the faith of Islam. They learned about it from Muslim spice traders who came to their countries from the Middle East.

NATURE GODS

AUSTRALASIA

In the islands of Hawaii, people worshiped spirits that they believed controlled waves, storms, and volcanoes. They made statues of them out of woven branches and built stone altars, where they offered sacrifices.

In Australia, Aborigines believed that long ago, in the Dreamtime, ancestors of all creatures wandered across the earth, linking everything together in a peaceful whole. The Aborigines held ceremonies at holy sites to recreate the ancestors' wanderings and to bring peace and order to the world.

▶ This Native American healer, called a shaman, was painted by John White about 1584. Shamans healed sick people and brought good fortune by being in touch with magic spirits. To do this, they chanted and danced until they fell into a trance.

FEEDING THE SUN

AMERICAS

The Aztecs of Mexico believed they had to offer prayers to the gods and feed them with human blood, or the world would come to an end. When they built a new temple in honor of the sun god, in the Aztec city of Tenochtitlán, more than 20,000 captives were sacrificed over several days.

▼ The Aztecs believed in many gods. This is the sun god, shown wearing a headdress of feathers.

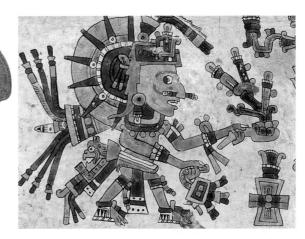

EARTH AND MOON

The Incas of South America also worshiped the sun and many other nature gods, including Mother Earth and Mother Moon. They honored the gods with singing and dancing, and offered sacrifices to them. They believed that if they did not do this, the gods would punish them by sending earthquakes or by making their crops die in the fields.

GUARDIAN SPIRITS

The Incas believed that everyone had a guardian spirit, which they called a huauqui. This belief was shared by many North American peoples, too. They went to a quiet place, where they prayed, fasted, and sometimes took drugs and hoped the spirit would contact them.

PEOPLES FROM AROUND THE WORLD

Aborigines   The first inhabitants of Australia, who arrived there about 40,000 years ago.

Aztec   A civilization in central Mexico, powerful from about 1300 to 1521, when it was conquered by the Spanish.

Bedouin   Nomads who lived in Arabia and the dry, desert lands of the Middle East. They bred camels and kept flocks of sheep and goats.

Chimu   A civilization in South America, conquered by the Incas about 1470.

Chinook   Native Americans who lived on the northwestern coast of North America. They lived by fishing for salmon and trading in shells.

Hopi   Native Americans from the semidesert regions of southwestern North America. Some of their village sites have been occupied continuously for about 1,000 years.

Inca   A civilization in the Andes Mountains of South America that was powerful from about 1200 to 1533, when it was conquered by the Spanish.

Inuit   Native Americans who arrived in the Arctic regions of North America about 4,000 years ago.

Maori   Settlers in New Zealand who came from the Pacific islands from about A.D. 800.

Mongols   Nomads who originally lived on the wide grassy plains north of China. Around 1200 they began to move south and west, conquering a vast empire. By Leonardo's time the Mongol Empire had been divided into four smaller, weaker kingdoms.

Native Americans   The first inhabitants of the Americas, who arrived there about 30,000 years ago. Native American people were divided into many groups with different lifestyles and languages.

Navajo   Native American hunters and gatherers who migrated from what is now Alaska and Canada to live as farmers in the dry semidesert lands of southwestern North America.

San   Hunters and gatherers who have lived in the deserts of southern Africa for thousands of years. By Leonardo's time some of their lands were occupied by Khoikhoi and Bantu-speaking people from the north.

Secotan   Native Americans who lived on the southeastern coast of North America. They grew crops of corn and hunted deer in the woods.

administrator   Someone who organizes and manages things.
anatomy   The study of the structure of animals and plants.
ancestor   A long-dead relative.
architecture   Style of buildings.
the arts   Music, art, and literature.
astronomy   The study of the sun, moon, planets, and stars.

blood transfusion   Giving one person blood taken from another.
Buddhism   A religion founded by the Buddha, an Indian prince who lived in India from about 563 to 483 B.C. He taught his followers to seek truth and the right way to live by meditation.

Christianity   A religion based on the teachings of Jesus Christ, who was executed around A.D. 30. Christians believe Jesus is the son of God.
the Church   The organization of the Christian religion. A church is a building where people worship.
citizen   A person who lives in a nation or city and has rights as a member of the community.
city-state   A city that rules itself and the surrounding countryside, villages, and farms.
civilization   A society with its own laws, customs, beliefs, and artistic traditions.
code   A collection of laws.
coral   A hard, often beautifully colored material formed by the skeletons of tiny sea animals.

diplomacy   Skill in dealing with people and governments.
dynasty   A ruling family.

earthwork A large mound, bank, or circle made of earth dug from the surrounding land.

engineer Someone who plans, designs, or builds new machines, roads, bridges, and so on.

frescoes Pictures painted directly on freshly plastered walls.

glazed Covered with a smooth, glassy coating. Glaze was used to make objects more beautiful.

governor The ruler of part of an empire or kingdom.

Hindu A person who follows the Hindu religion, which developed in India between about 1500–600 B.C. Hindus worship many gods.

Holy Roman Emperor The title of the ruler of the Holy Roman Empire, located in western and central Europe.

irrigate To channel water into dry land, so crops can grow there.

Islam The worship of Allah (God), taught by Muhammad, a prophet who lived in Arabia from A.D. 570–632. Followers of Islam are called Muslims.

Jains People who follow the teachings of Mahavira, a holy man who lived in the sixth century B.C. Jains try not to harm any person, bird, animal, insect, or plant.

jester An entertainer who made people laugh.

looted Stolen by an invading army.

manuscript A book written and beautifully decorated by hand.

meditation Thinking deeply about spiritual things.

merchant A person who buys and sells goods.

Middle East The area that stretches eastwards from the Mediterranean Sea towards Asia.

missionary A person who travels to another country to teach about his or her religious beliefs.

mosque A building where Muslims pray and worship.

Muslim A follower of the religion of Islam.

nomads People who have no settled home and who move from place to place in search of food, water, and grazing land.

oba A king from the African kingdom of Benin.

Parsees People who follow the teachings of Zoroaster, who lived in Persia around 600 B.C. Parsees worship Ahura Mazda and see the world as a battleground between good and evil forces.

patron Someone who spends money to pay for new works of art, music, or literature.

pearl oyster A shellfish that produces pearls by coating anything that gets into its shell with a beautiful, shiny coating, called nacre.

peasant A person, usually poor, who lives and works in the countryside.

philosophy The study of ideas, knowledge, and wisdom.

plaque A flat decorated tablet with a picture, writing, or carving on it, often on a wall.

ransom Money demanded by soldiers or criminals as payment for setting prisoners free.

Reformation A religious movement, strong in northern Europe in the 1500s. Religious reformers wanted freedom to worship in their own way and to reform the Roman Catholic Church.

Renaissance A period in the 1400s and 1500s when people explored new ideas and artistic styles. A typical Renaissance scholar was interested in all areas of knowledge, including art, science, music, and travel.

republic A place ruled by elected leaders, not by a king or queen.

ritual Traditional way of marking a special, often religious, event.

Roman Catholic The Christian church headed by the Pope in Rome, Italy.

sauna A hot steam bath.

scholar A learned person who often studies.

sultan A Muslim ruler.

taxes Payments made to a government or ruler to pay for running the country.

technology The science of developing tools and techniques to meet practical needs.

terra cotta Clay that has been baked in a special oven called a kiln at a fairly low temperature. It is usually a brown-red color.

tolerant (of religion) Allowing people to follow their own faith and worship in their own way.

trade route A long-distance route used by traveling merchants.

trading post A place where merchants meet to trade.

tribute Money or goods paid to rulers by conquered people.

INDEX